Shark Tales

PATHFINDER EDITION

By Rene Ebersole

CONTENTS

By Rene Ebersole

Shark

Sharks are in trouble. Some kinds may die out in the near future.

Tales

Hammerhead shark

What would you do if a hungry shark attacked you? Hopefully you will never have to answer that question for real. Aaron Perez (above) wasn't so lucky because one summer, as the 11-year-old was wading in the Gulf of Mexico, a bull shark suddenly attacked him.

Fortunately, Aaron knew what to do because, just the day before, he had learned that one should punch an attacking shark in the gills or eyes.

As the bull shark bit down on the boy's arm, Perez punched it in the gills. The shark let go, and Aaron managed to get to shore safely.

Who's Afraid of Whom?

Aaron survived the attack and a few days later, he talked about it. "The shark was big and ugly," he said, "bigger than my dad."

Shark attacks are nasty, but luckily, they are also rare. Worldwide, sharks attack fewer than a hundred people a year and only about six die.

Most attacks happen in waters where sharks are known to live. In such places, the toothy hunters can scare many people away from the beach. Overall, though, sharks have far more reason to fear us than we have to fear them.

Shark Hunts

Each year, humans kill 60 million sharks. A key reason is to get shark **cartilage**, which is the soft, flexible material that makes up a shark's skeleton.

Many people use shark cartilage to treat cancer, and you can find it in some U.S. health food stores. But no one has proven that shark cartilage actually cures cancer.

People also want shark fins. Chefs in many Asian countries use the fins to make soup. The tasty soup is very expensive. In China, a single bowl can cost a hundred dollars!

Beach Bullies. *Bull sharks live in shallow water and can attack humans.*

Overhunting

Because some shark parts are so valuable, a few species, or kinds, are overhunted, which could cause them to die out forever. That would be too bad. Why? Well, sharks have a long history on Earth, and our world wouldn't be the same without them.

The first sharks lived 400 million years ago, which was long before the dinosaurs. Little is known about **prehistoric** sharks because scientists have found few fossils. That's because cartilage doesn't last long. But scientists do find one thing—teeth.

Prehistoric shark tooth

Modern great white shark tooth

All Sorts of Sharks

Roughly 400 shark species swim in the world's oceans today, and they come in all sizes. By and large, sharks are **predators,** which means they eat other animals. Now let's meet a few sharks.

The whale shark is the largest fish in the sea, and when it's fully grown, it can be as long as a school bus. Yet it does not hunt large animals. This shark swims with its mouth wide open instead to gather anchovies, sardines, and tiny animals and plants called plankton.

An angel shark hides in sand and mud on the seafloor, and when a school of fish swims by, the shark snatches dinner with its jaws.

The hammerhead shark uses its head to pin down **prey,** or food, while eating.

The saw shark has a snout that looks like a saw blade, which it uses to sweep the sand until it finds a meal.

Nearly 5,000 razor-sharp teeth line the mouth of a great white shark. When one falls out, another replaces it. Those teeth help the shark hunt, and yet it doesn't chew its food. It gulps.

Great whites get blamed for most shark attacks. Tiger and bull sharks can also be dangerous. So can a few other species.

Why Sharks Attack

No one knows why sharks attack people. Scientists say that it may be a case of mistaken identity because to a shark, a swimmer can look like a seal. Many sharks eat seals.

Tourism may be a bigger problem. Many people want to see sharks up close, so they dump **chum**, or fish parts, into the sea. Hungry sharks then swim toward the tourists'

In Hot Water. *Great white sharks look anything but endangered, and yet their numbers are dropping around the world.*

boats. Sharks may learn to go to the same places again and again to find food.

Sharks may not even like how people taste. Scientists point out that sharks often leave after just one bite. Of course, even a single shark bite can be deadly.

Deep Trouble

As deadly as some sharks look, the fearsome fish are not unstoppable. Nearly 80 shark species are threatened or endangered, which means they may die out.

"Time is running out for these species," says Sonja Fordham, a scientist at the Ocean Conservancy. "Programs to protect sharks and their habitat are urgently needed to ensure that these magnificent species survive."

© Gérard Lacz/AgeFotostock (GREAT WHITE); WILLIAM H. BOND (ART); PHOTODISC (FISH)

Wordwise

cartilage: soft, flexible material that makes up a shark's skeleton
chum: fish parts
predator: animal that eats other animals
prehistoric: before recorded history
prey: animal eaten by another animal

Meet the Sharks

Great White Shark
18 feet

Tiger Shark
15 feet

Dusky Shark
10 feet

Hammerhead Shark
15 feet

Shortfin Mako
12 feet

Bull Shark
9 feet

Spiny Dogfish
4 feet

Sixgill Shark
17 feet

Leopard Shark
4 feet

Greenland Shark
18 feet

WILLIAM H. BOND

Some 400 shark species navigate the world's oceans. You've probably heard of only a few of these creatures of the deep. That's because different sharks live in different parts of the sea. Some swim near the shore, while others dwell in deeper waters.

Sharks also come in different sizes. The whale shark is the largest fish, and it is nearly the size of a school bus. The smallest sharks are only a few inches long. Some of Earth's sharks are below. How are these sharks alike, and how are they different?

Whale Shark
40 feet

Basking Shark
25 feet

Lemon Shark
10 feet

Porbeagle
8 feet

Sand Tiger Shark
10 feet

Silky Shark
9 feet

Blue Shark
9 feet

Blacktip Shark
8 feet

Oceanic Whitetip Shark
10 feet

Soupfin Shark
6 feet

Sandbar Shark
7 feet

Thresher Shark
15 feet

Swell Shark
3 feet

Horn Shark
4 feet

Angel Shark
4 feet

Nurse Shark
10 feet

Shark Teeth

Cutting Edge. *The teeth of this great white shark have jagged edges that can quickly cut and crush their meals.*

Scientists can tell a lot about a shark just by looking at its teeth. They can tell what kind of shark it was, how large it grew, and even what it liked to eat.

You see, each kind of shark has its favorite foods. Some species adore the taste of octopus and squid, while others snack on fish, turtles, or birds. With such varied diets, sharks need different kinds of teeth. Some species have long, thin teeth, which are perfect for nabbing small fish. Others have sturdy teeth that help them wrestle with larger prey. These are strong enough to chomp through muscle and bone.

The most amazing thing about sharks is just how many teeth they have—and how many they lose. People get only two sets of teeth to last a lifetime, but sharks come with up to 15 sets. It's a good thing, too, since their teeth are always falling out. When one tooth drops out, another simply slides into place, so sharks can lose as many as 50,000 teeth in their lifetime!

Look at the shark teeth below. What can you tell about the shape of each tooth?

TOOTH TYPES

This sand tiger tooth is long and pointy, which helps a shark stab into small, bony fish and eels.

This tooth from a great white shark has an edge like a saw, which helps with cutting and tearing.

This sharp, triangular tooth, which comes from a bull shark, is good for slicing into large prey.

WILLIAM H. BOND

SharkTales

Bite into these questions and see how much you've learned.

1 Why do people hunt and kill sharks?

2 Why is it hard to learn about ancient sharks?

3 What do sharks eat?

4 What are some ways that sharks catch and eat their prey?

5 Why might sharks attack people?